SHIRLEY WILLIS was born in Glasgow, Scotland. She has worked as an illustrator, designer, and editor, mainly on books for children.

BETTY ROOT was the Director of the Reading and Language Information Center at the University of Reading, England, for over twenty years. She has worked on numerous children's books, both fiction and non-fiction.

PETER LAFFERTY is a former secondary school science teacher. Since 1985 he has been a full-time author of science and technology books for children and family audiences. He has edited and contributed to many scientific encyclopedias and dictionaries.

BOOK EDITOR: KAREN BARKER SMITH
EDITORIAL ASSISTANT: STEPHANIE COLE
TECHNICAL CONSULTANT: PETER LAFFERTY
LANGUAGE CONSULTANT: BETTY ROOT

AN SBC BOOK, CONCEIVED, EDITED AND DESIGNED BY
THE SALARIYA BOOK COMPANY, 25, MARLBOROUGH PLACE,
BRIGHTON, EAST SUSSEX BN1 1UB, UNITED KINGDOM.
© THE SALARIYA BOOK COMPANY LTD MCMXCIX

FIRST AMERICAN EDITION 1999 BY FRANKLIN WATTS
GROLIER PUBLISHING CO., INC., 90 SHERMAN TURNPIKE, DANBURY CT 06816

ISBN 0-531-11828-2 (LIB. BDG.)
ISBN 0-531-15978-7 (PBK.)

VISIT FRANKLIN WATTS ON THE INTERNET AT :HTTP://PUBLISHING.GROLIER.COM

GROLIER
PUBLISHING

A catalog record for this title is available from the Library of Congress.

WHIZ KIDS

CONTENTS

Wherever you see this sign, ask an adult to help you.

WHIZ KIDS
TELL ME HOW SHIPS FLOAT

Written and illustrated by
SHIRLEY WILLIS

W
FRANKLIN WATTS
A Division of Grolier Publishing
NEW YORK • LONDON • HONG KONG • SYDNEY
DANBURY, CONNECTICUT

WILL IT FLOAT OR SINK?

Some objects float.
Some objects sink.
Some objects float so low
in the water that they look
like they are sinking.

A pencil floats.
A fork sinks.
A lemon floats
low in the water.

READY, SET, SPLASH!

Fill a large bowl with water and collect some objects to test. Try to find things that are different shapes and sizes — some can be heavy and some light. Look for things made from different materials. Before you drop each one in the water, guess if it will sink or float.
Are you right?

SPLASH!

PLOP!

ARE FLOATERS BIG OR SMALL?

If an object is light,
it will float.
It can be big or small.

WILL IT FLOAT...OR SINK?

FLOATERS AND SINKERS

Golf balls and Ping-Pong balls are the same shape and size. If you drop them in water, one sinks and the other floats.
The golf ball is small but heavy
— it sinks.
The Ping-Pong ball is small but light
— it floats.

WHY DOES IT FLOAT?

A soccer ball is much bigger than a golf ball, but the soccer ball is light, so it floats.

A SOCCER BALL IS BIG, BUT IT FLOATS!

CAN I FLOAT?

The air inside your body
helps you float.
Air makes you lighter.

When something
is filled with air,
it floats.

BREATHE IN

We breathe with
our lungs. As you
breathe in, you fill
your lungs with air.
The air inside you
helps you float in
the same way
that air-filled
water wings do.

your
lungs

10

SEE FOR YOURSELF

Take two water wings, but
only blow up one of them.
Now try to push them both
under the water.
It's hard to push the water wing
that is full of air underwater.

WHY DO THINGS FLOAT?

When something falls into water,
the water tries to push it
back out again.
The water's push
is called upthrust.

THE UPTHRUST KEEPS PUSHING IT OUT AGAIN!

If an object floats,
it's hard to push it
underwater.

If an object is light, the upthrust can push it back up to the top of the water — it floats.

GOING UP?

A block of wood floats. You can make it sink by putting some coins on it. If you flick the coins off one by one, it will float again. The wood hasn't moved by itself — the water's upthrust has pushed it back up to the top of the water.

13

WHY DO STONES SINK?

A stone sinks because it is heavy.
The upthrust tries to push it
back up, but the stone
weighs too much.

The upthrust is
not strong enough
to push the stone up
to the top of the water.

AN APPLE
IS LIGHT!

A STONE
IS HEAVY!

BIG STONES SINK!

All stones sink because they are too heavy to float.

SMALL STONES SINK!

15

WHY DID THE BATHTUB OVERFLOW?

If you put too much water in the bathtub, it will overflow when you get in.

SEE FOR YOURSELF

Fill the bathtub halfway.
Mark the water level with a crayon.
Now climb in.
What happens to the water level?

16

When you get into a bathtub,
you take up some of the water's space.
Your body pushes the bathwater
out of its way.
As you get in,
the water level rises.

When any object is put
into water, it pushes the
water out of its way.
The water and the object
can't both be in the same
place at the same time,
so the water level rises.

DO ICEBERGS SINK OR FLOAT?

An iceberg is like a mountain of ice that floats in the sea.
Only the top of an iceberg can be seen — most of it is underwater.

SEE HOW IT FLOATS

Fill a glass halfway with water. Now drop in an ice cube.
See how much of it floats below the water.
This is exactly how a huge iceberg looks as it floats in the sea.

18

WHOOSH!

If an object is light, it will float. Ice floats, but just barely — it floats very low in the water.
This is why so much of an iceberg is hidden underwater.

19

IF STONES SINK, WHY DO SHIPS FLOAT?

A ship made of steel is very heavy, but its shape helps it float. The hollow space inside a ship looks empty, but it is full of air. The air inside the ship makes it lighter and helps it float.

DOES IT WORK?

Fill a bowl with water.
Find some small metal
objects like keys, coins,
forks, or spoons.
Drop them in the water
and they will sink.
Place a large cooking
pot in the water
and it floats.
The pot is heavier
— why does it float?

(The air inside the pot
makes it light enough to
float.)

21

IS THE SHAPE IMPORTANT?

A boat's shape takes up
a lot of space in the water.
The boat pushes lots of water
out of its way.

Pushing so much water aside
makes more upthrust.
The water's upthrust
is so strong that
the boat floats.

CAN YOU MAKE IT FLOAT?

You will need: A bowl of water
Some modeling clay made
into two equal-sized balls
A key

1. Make one ball of modeling clay into a cupped boat shape and place it carefully in the water.
2. Now put the other ball of modeling clay in the water.
3. One sinks and one floats — why?

The boat shape floats because it is lighter (it's full of air). The boat shape makes more upthrust than the ball of modeling clay.

Now place the key very gently in your boat. Can you make the key float too?

NOW IT FLOATS!

23

WHY DO BOATS SINK?

A boat with a heavy load
floats low in the water.
A boat that is overloaded
floats too low in the water.
If water comes into the boat,
it will sink.

This boat weighs
too much, so it is
too low in the water.
When water comes
into the boat,
the boat gets
heavier and sinks.

A special mark on the side of a ship shows if it is too low in the water. The mark is called the Plimsoll line.

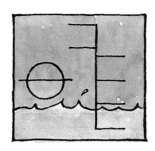

HOW MUCH IS TOO MUCH?

You will need: A small plastic box (this is your boat)
A crayon
Some pebbles

1. Float the "boat" in water. Use the crayon to mark how high the water comes up its side.
2. Place some pebbles in the boat.
3. Mark the water level again.
4. Slowly add more pebbles. The boat gets lower and lower. How many pebbles sink the boat?

WE'RE SINKING!

WHAT FLOATS AND SINKS?

A submarine can float and sink.
A submarine is a ship
that can travel on water
or underneath it.
It must be waterproof
to keep water out
when it dives underwater.

26

A submarine has to carry
bottles of air on board
or its crew will run out of
air to breathe.

SOME SUBMARINES
CAN STAY UNDERWATER
FOR MONTHS!

HOW DO SUBMARINES WORK?

A submarine can change
how much it weighs.
This makes it rise
or sink in the water.

Fill one balloon with water
and another with air.
Can you feel the difference?

BALLAST TANKS

These are special tanks
inside a submarine. By
filling them with water,
the submarine gets
heavier. By filling them
with air, it gets lighter.

THIS BALLOON
IS LIGHT — IT'S
FULL OF AIR!

THIS BALLOON
IS HEAVY — IT'S
FULL OF WATER!

GOING DOWN

The tanks are flooded with water to make the submarine too heavy to float. It can then dive underwater.

RAISE THE SUBMARINE

You will need: A plastic bottle
       A piece of plastic tubing
1. Fill the bottle with water.
2. Put one end of the tube inside it.
3. Place it carefully into a bowl of water.
4. Slowly blow into the tube to make the bottle rise.

This is how a submarine works.

GOING UP

Air is pumped back into the tanks to force the water out. The air in the tanks makes the submarine light enough to float. It rises to the top of the water again.

29

GLOSSARY

ballast tanks Special tanks that can be made heavier or lighter to make a submarine sink or rise.

float When an object rests on top of water.

heavy When an object weighs a lot.

hollow When an object has empty space inside it.

iceberg A huge piece of ice that floats in the sea.

light When an object weighs very little.

lungs The parts of your body that fill with air when you breathe.

overflow When something spills over the top of its container.

overload When too much is carried.

Plimsoll line A mark on the side of a ship to show if it is overloaded.

sink When an object disappears below the water.

submarine A ship that can travel on or under water.

upthrust The force when water pushes upward.

water level The height of the water.

waterproof Sealed to keep water on the outside.

INDEX